USA
NATIONAL PARKS

LET'S EXPLORE THE WILD

THIS OUTDOOR ADVENTURE JOURNAL

& PASSPORT STAMP BOOK BELONGS TO :

_____

Special request

Thank you for your trust. Your satisfaction means the world to me and I hope this USA National Parks Adventure Journal will meet your expectations.

I am a small independent author : if you enjoy this book, please take a few minutes to leave me a review on Amazon. Each one of your reviews is really important to support my work and help me provide you with new quality books.

Thank you !

Amy Birdwhistle

USA National Parks Journal & Log Book

© Copyright 2020 by Amy Birdwhistle. All rights reserved.

This publication is protected by copyright. No part of this book may be copied, reproduced or redistributed in any form without the express written consent and permission by the author.

U.S. NATIONAL PARKS

① ACADIA
② AMERICAN SAMOA
③ ARCHES
④ BADLANDS
⑤ BIG BEND
⑥ BISCAYNE
⑦ BLACK CANYON OF THE GUNNISON
⑧ BRYCE CANYON
⑨ CANYONLANDS
⑩ CAPITOL REEF
⑪ CARLSBAD CAVERNS
⑫ CHANNEL ISLANDS
⑬ CONGAREE
⑭ CRATER LAKE
⑮ CUYAHOGA VALLEY
⑯ DEATH VALLEY
⑰ DENALI
⑱ DRY TORTUGAS
⑲ EVERGLADES
⑳ GATES OF THE ARCTIC
㉑ GATEWAY ARCH
㉒ GLACIER
㉓ GLACIER BAY
㉔ GRAND CANYON
㉕ GRAND TETON
㉖ GREAT BASIN
㉗ GREAT SAND DUNES
㉘ GREAT SMOKY MOUNTAINS
㉙ GUADALUPE MOUNTAINS
㉚ HALEAKALĀ
㉛ HAWAI'I VOLCANOES
㉜ HOT SPRINGS
㉝ INDIANA DUNES
㉞ ISLE ROYALE
㉟ JOSHUA TREE
㊱ KATMAI
㊲ KENAI FJORDS
㊳ KINGS CANYON
㊴ KOBUK VALLEY
㊵ LAKE CLARK
㊶ LASSEN VOCALNIC
㊷ MAMMOTH CAVE
㊸ MESA VERDE
㊹ MOUNT RAINIER
㊺ NORTH CASCADES
㊻ OLYMPIC
㊼ PETRIFIED FOREST
㊽ PINNACLES
㊾ RED WOOD
㊿ ROCKY MOUNTAIN
(51) SAGUARO
(52) SEQUOIA
(53) SHENANDOAH
(54) THEODORE ROOSEVELT
(55) VIRGIN ISLANDS
(56) VOYAGEURS
(57) WHITE SANDS
(58) WIND CAVE
(59) WRANGELL-ST.ELIAS
(60) YELLOWSTONE
(61) YOSEMITE
(62) ZION

U.S. NATIONAL PARKS CHECKLIST & TRACKING LOG

	U.S. NATIONAL PARK	LOCATION	ESTABLISHED	DATE(S) VISITED
○	ACADIA	MAINE	1919	
○	AMERICAN SAMOA	AMERICAN SAMOA	1988	
○	ARCHES	UTAH	1971	
○	BADLANDS	SOUTH DAKOTA	1978	
○	BIG BEND	TEXAS	1944	
○	BISCAYNE	FLORIDA	1980	
○	BLACK CANYON OF THE GUNNISON	COLORADO	1999	
○	BRYCE CANYON	UTAH	1928	
○	CANYONLANDS	UTAH	1964	
○	CAPITOL REEF	UTAH	1971	
○	CARLSBAD CAVERNS	NEW MEXICO	1930	
○	CHANNEL ISLANDS	CALIFORNIA	1980	
○	CONGAREE	SOUTH CAROLINA	2003	
○	CRATER LAKE	OREGON	1902	
○	CUYAHOGA VALLEY	OHIO	2000	
○	DEATH VALLEY	CALIFORNIA/NEVADA	1994	
○	DENALI	ALASKA	1917	
○	DRY TORTUGAS	FLORIDA	1992	
○	EVERGLADES	FLORIDA	1934	
○	GATES OF THE ARCTIC	ALASKA	1980	
○	GATEWAY ARCH	MISSOURI	2018	
○	GLACIER	MONTANA	1910	
○	GLACIER BAY	ALASKA	1980	
○	GRAND CANYON	ARIZONA	1919	
○	GRAND TETON	WYOMING	1929	
○	GREAT BASIN	NEVADA	1986	
○	GREAT SAND DUNES	COLORADO	2004	
○	GREAT SMOKY MOUNTAINS	TENNESSEE/NORTH CAROLINA	1934	
○	GUADALUPE MOUNTAINS	TEXAS	1966	
○	HALEAKALĀ	HAWAII	1916	
○	HAWAI'I VOLCANOES	HAWAII	1916	

U.S. NATIONAL PARKS CHECKLIST & TRACKING LOG

	U.S. NATIONAL PARK	LOCATION	ESTABLISHED	DATE(S) VISITED
○	**HOT SPRINGS**	ARKANSAS	1921	
○	**INDIANA DUNES**	INDIANA	2019	
○	**ISLE ROYALE**	MICHIGAN	1940	
○	**JOSHUA TREE**	CALIFORNIA	1994	
○	**KATMAI**	ALASKA	1980	
○	**KENAI FJORDS**	ALASKA	1980	
○	**KINGS CANYON**	CALIFORNIA	1940	
○	**KOBUK VALLEY**	ALASKA	1980	
○	**LAKE CLARK**	ALASKA	1980	
○	**LASSEN VOCALNIC**	CALIFORNIA	1916	
○	**MAMMOTH CAVE**	KENTUCKY	1941	
○	**MESA VERDE**	COLORADO	1906	
○	**MOUNT RAINIER**	WASHINGTON	1899	
○	**NORTH CASCADES**	WASHINGTON	1968	
○	**OLYMPIC**	WASHINGTON	1938	
○	**PETRIFIED FOREST**	ARIZONA	1962	
○	**PINNACLES**	CALIFORNIA	2013	
○	**RED WOOD**	CALIFORNIA	1968	
○	**ROCKY MOUNTAIN**	COLORADO	1915	
○	**SAGUARO**	ARIZONA	1994	
○	**SEQUOIA**	CALIFORNIA	1890	
○	**SHENANDOAH**	VIRGINIA	1935	
○	**THEODORE ROOSEVELT**	NORTH DAKOTA	1978	
○	**VIRGIN ISLANDS**	U.S. VIRGIN ISLANDS	1956	
○	**VOYAGEURS**	MINNESOTA	1971	
○	**WHITE SANDS**	NEW MEXICO	2019	
○	**WIND CAVE**	SOUTH DAKOTA	1903	
○	**WRANGELL-ST.ELIAS**	ALASKA	1980	
○	**YELLOWSTONE**	WYOMING/MONTANA/IDAHO	1872	
○	**YOSEMITE**	CALIFORNIA	1890	
○	**ZION**	UTAH	1919	

ACADIA
NATIONAL PARK

○ CITY/STATE ENTERED:

📅 DATE(S) VISITED:

WEATHER:
°F

👥 COMPANIONS:

⛺ LODGING:

💵 FEE(S):

🥾 FAVORITE MOMENT:

⛰ SIGHTS :

🦅 WILDLIFE OBSERVED:

POPULAR ATTRACTIONS I VISITED/EXPERIENCED:

- ☐ CADILLAC MOUNTAIN
- ☐ SAND BEACH
- ☐ JORDAN POND
- ☐ OTTER CLIFF
- ☐ THUNDER HOLE
- ☐ BAR ISLAND TRAIL
- ☐ BUBBLE ROCK
- ☐ GORHAM MOUNTAIN TRAIL
- ☐ BEEHIVE TRAIL
- ☐ BASS HARBOR HEAD LIGHTHOUSE

OVERALL EXPERIENCE
☆

10

NATIONAL PARK OF
AMERICAN SAMOA

◎ CITY/STATE ENTERED:

📅 DATE(S) VISITED:

WEATHER:
°F

👥 **COMPANIONS:**

🏕 **LODGING:**

💰 **FEE(S):**

🥾 **FAVORITE MOMENT:**

⛰ **SIGHTS :**

🐦 **WILDLIFE OBSERVED:**

POPULAR ATTRACTIONS I VISITED/EXPERIENCED:

- ☐ OFU ISLAND CORAL LAGOON
- ☐ LAUFUTI FALLS
- ☐ LUATELE CRATER
- ☐ POLA ISLAND
- ☐ SAMOAN FAMILY HOMESTAY
- ☐ LATA MOUNTAIN
- ☐ MOUNT'ALAVA SUMMIT
- ☐ OGE BEACH
- ☐ TAFEU COVE
- ☐ VAI'AVA STRAIT

OVERALL EXPERIENCE
☆

10

ARCHES
NATIONAL PARK

⦿ CITY/STATE ENTERED:

🗓 DATE(S) VISITED:

WEATHER: 🚩 ☀ ⛅ 🌧 ⛈ ❄
_____ °F

👥 COMPANIONS:

🏕 LODGING:

💵 FEE(S):

🥾 FAVORITE MOMENT:

⛰ SIGHTS :

🐦 WILDLIFE OBSERVED:

POPULAR ATTRACTIONS I VISITED/EXPERIENCED:

- ☐ FIERY FURNACE
- ☐ LANDSCAPE ARCH
- ☐ DELICATE ARCH
- ☐ DOUBLE ARCH
- ☐ PARK AVENUE TRAIL
- ☐ COURTHOUSE TOWERS VIEWPOINT
- ☐ DEVILS GARDEN TRAILHEAD
- ☐ THE WINDOWS
- ☐ SAND DUNE ARCH
- ☐ BALANCED ROCK

OVERALL EXPERIENCE

☆

10

BADLANDS
NATIONAL PARK

📍 CITY/STATE ENTERED:

📅 DATE(S) VISITED:

WEATHER:
_____ °F

👥 COMPANIONS:

⛺ LODGING:

💵 FEE(S):

🥾 FAVORITE MOMENT:

⛰ SIGHTS :

🐦 WILDLIFE OBSERVED:

POPULAR ATTRACTIONS I VISITED/EXPERIENCED:

- [ ] BADLANDS WALL
- [ ] PANORAMA POINT
- [ ] ROBERTS PRAIRIE DOG TOWN
- [ ] BID BADLANDS OVERLOOK
- [ ] SADDLE PASS TRAIL
- [ ] BADLANDS LOOP ROAD
- [ ] DOOR TRAIL
- [ ] NOTCH TRAIL
- [ ] YELLOW MOUNDS OVERLOOK
- [ ] CLIFF SHELF NATURE TRAIL

OVERALL EXPERIENCE

☆

10

BIG BEND
NATIONAL PARK

○ CITY/STATE ENTERED:

📅 DATE(S) VISITED:

WEATHER: 🚩 ☀️ ⛅ 🌧️ ⛈️ ❄️
_____ °F

COMPANIONS:

LODGING:

FEE(S):

FAVORITE MOMENT:

SIGHTS:

WILDLIFE OBSERVED:

POPULAR ATTRACTIONS I VISITED/EXPERIENCED:

- [ ] ROSS MAXWELL SCENIC DRIVE
- [ ] MULE EARS SPRING TRAIL
- [ ] BOQUILLAS CANYON TRAIL
- [ ] LOST MINE TRAIL
- [ ] FOSSIL DISCOVERY EXHIBIT
- [ ] SANTA ELENA CANYON
- [ ] LANGFORD HOT SPRINGS
- [ ] WINDOW VIEW TRAIL
- [ ] CHISOS BASIN LOOP
- [ ] RIO GRANDE NATURE TRAIL

OVERALL EXPERIENCE
☆

10

BISCAYNE
NATIONAL PARK

⬤ CITY/STATE ENTERED:

DATE(S) VISITED:

WEATHER:
___ °F

COMPANIONS:

LODGING:

FEE(S):

FAVORITE MOMENT:

SIGHTS:

WILDLIFE OBSERVED:

POPULAR ATTRACTIONS I VISITED/EXPERIENCED:

- [ ] SANDS KEY
- [ ] SPITE TRAIL
- [ ] MARITIME HERITAGE TRAIL
- [ ] ELLIOTT KEY
- [ ] MANGROVE FORESTS
- [ ] ADAMS KEY
- [ ] BOCA CHITA KEY
- [ ] STILTSVILLE
- [ ] JONES FAMILY HISTORIC DISTRICT & LAGOON
- [ ] SNORKELING/PADDLING

OVERALL EXPERIENCE

☆

10

BLACK CANYON OF THE GUNNISON NATIONAL PARK

○ CITY/STATE ENTERED:

DATE(S) VISITED:

WEATHER: °F

COMPANIONS:

LODGING:

FEE(S):

FAVORITE MOMENT:

SIGHTS:

WILDLIFE OBSERVED:

POPULAR ATTRACTIONS I VISITED/EXPERIENCED:

- [ ] PULPIT ROCK OVERLOOK
- [ ] PAINTED WALL
- [ ] TOMICHI POINT
- [ ] SOUTH RIM DRIVE
- [ ] GREEN MOUNTAIN SUMMIT
- [ ] WARNER POINT NATURE TRAIL
- [ ] NORTH VISTA TRAIL TO EXCLAMATION POINT
- [ ] GUNNISON POINT OVERLOOK
- [ ] OAK FLAT LOOP TRAIL
- [ ] EAST PORTAL ROAD

OVERALL EXPERIENCE

☆

10

BRYCE CANYON
NATIONAL PARK

○ CITY/STATE ENTERED:

DATE(S) VISITED:

WEATHER:
°F

👥 **COMPANIONS:**

🏕 **LODGING:**

💵 **FEE(S):**

🥾 **FAVORITE MOMENT:**

⛰ **SIGHTS :**

🐦 **WILDLIFE OBSERVED:**

🌲 **POPULAR ATTRACTIONS I VISITED/EXPERIENCED:**

- [ ] INSPIRATION POINT
- [ ] SUNRISE POINT
- [ ] FAIRYLAND POINT
- [ ] SUNSET POINT
- [ ] NAVAJO LOOP TRAIL
- [ ] BRYCE POINT
- [ ] BRYCE CANYON SCENIC DRIVE
- [ ] PEEK-A-BOO TRAIL
- [ ] QUEEN'S GARDEN TRAIL
- [ ] NATURAL BRIDGE

OVERALL EXPERIENCE

☆

10

CANYONLAMDS
NATIONAL PARK

○ CITY/STATE ENTERED:

📅 DATE(S) VISITED:

WEATHER:
🚩 ☀️ ⛅ 🌧️ ⛈️ ❄️
_____ °F

👥 COMPANIONS:

⛺ LODGING:

💵 FEE(S):

🥾 FAVORITE MOMENT:

⛰️ SIGHTS :

🐦 WILDLIFE OBSERVED:

POPULAR ATTRACTIONS I VISITED/EXPERIENCED:

- [ ] MESA ARCH
- [ ] WHALE ROCK TRAIL
- [ ] WHITE RIM TRAIL
- [ ] GREEN RIVER OVERLOOK
- [ ] HORSESHOE CANYON
- [ ] BUCK CANYON OVERLOOK
- [ ] GRAND VIEW POINT
- [ ] SHAFER CANYON OVERLOOK & TRAIL
- [ ] CAVE SPRING
- [ ] UPHEAVAL DOME

OVERALL EXPERIENCE
☆

10

CAPITOL REEF
NATIONAL PARK

◉ CITY/STATE ENTERED:

DATE(S) VISITED:

WEATHER:

_____ °F

COMPANIONS:

LODGING:

FEE(S):

FAVORITE MOMENT:

SIGHTS :

WILDLIFE OBSERVED:

POPULAR ATTRACTIONS I VISITED/EXPERIENCED:

- ☐ PIONEER REGISTER TRAIL
- ☐ CAPITOL GORGE TRAIL
- ☐ CASSIDY ARCH
- ☐ GOOSENECKS OVERLOOK
- ☐ PANORAMA POINT
- ☐ HICKMAN BRIDGE TRAIL
- ☐ BURR TRAIL ROAD
- ☐ FRUITA
- ☐ PETROGLYPH PANEL
- ☐ SULPHUR CREEK TRAIL

OVERALL EXPERIENCE

☆

10

CARLSBAD CAVERNS
NATIONAL PARK

◉ CITY/STATE ENTERED:

📅 DATE(S) VISITED:

WEATHER:
🚩 ☀️ ⛅ 🌧️ ⛈️ ❄️
_____ °F

👥 COMPANIONS:

🏕️ LODGING:

💵 FEE(S):

🥾 FAVORITE MOMENT:

🏔️ SIGHTS:

🦅 WILDLIFE OBSERVED:

🏞️ POPULAR ATTRACTIONS I VISITED/EXPERIENCED:

- [ ] NATURAL ENTRANCE TRAIL
- [ ] BAT FLIGHT PROGRAM
- [ ] GIANT DOME
- [ ] SLAUGHTER CANYON TRAIL
- [ ] HALL OF THE WHITE GIANT TOUR
- [ ] KING'S PALACE TOUR
- [ ] BIG ROOM TRAIL
- [ ] LOWER CAVE TOUR
- [ ] WALNUT CANYON DESERT DRIVE
- [ ] RATTLESNAKE SPRINGS

OVERALL EXPERIENCE
☆

10

CHANNEL ISLANDS
NATIONAL PARK

○ CITY/STATE ENTERED:

DATE(S) VISITED:

WEATHER:
_____ °F

COMPANIONS:

LODGING:

FEE(S):

FAVORITE MOMENT:

SIGHTS :

WILDLIFE OBSERVED:

POPULAR ATTRACTIONS I VISITED/EXPERIENCED:

- [ ] ANACAPA ISLAND
- [ ] INSPIRATION POINT
- [ ] NATIONAL MARINE SANCTUARY
- [ ] SANTA ROSA ISLAND
- [ ] EAST ANACAPA ISLAND TRAIL
- [ ] SANTA BARBARA ISLAND
- [ ] SANTA CRUZ ISLAND
- [ ] CAVERN POINT LOOP TRAIL
- [ ] SAN MIGUEL ISLAND
- [ ] SEA CAVES

OVERALL EXPERIENCE

☆

10

CONGAREE
NATIONAL PARK
• • • • •
📍 CITY/STATE ENTERED:

📅 DATE(S) VISITED:

WEATHER:
🚩 ☀️ ⛅ 🌧️ ⛈️ ❄️
_____ °F

👥 COMPANIONS:

🏕️ LODGING:

💰 FEE(S):

🥾 FAVORITE MOMENT:

⛰️ SIGHTS:

🐦 WILDLIFE OBSERVED:

POPULAR ATTRACTIONS I VISITED/EXPERIENCED:

- ☐ OAKRIDGE TRAIL
- ☐ BOARDWALK LOOP TRAIL
- ☐ BLUFF TRAIL
- ☐ CEDAR CREEK CANOE TRAIL
- ☐ POINSETT STATE PARK
- ☐ WESTON LAKE LOOP TRAIL
- ☐ NATURE DISCOVERY WALK
- ☐ KINGSNAKE TRAIL
- ☐ SYNCHRONOUS FIREFLIES
- ☐ MILLFORD PLANTATION HISTORIC SITE

OVERALL EXPERIENCE
☆

10

CRATER LAKE NATIONAL PARK

○ CITY/STATE ENTERED:

DATE(S) VISITED:

WEATHER:
_____ °F

COMPANIONS:

LODGING:

FEE(S):

FAVORITE MOMENT:

SIGHTS :

WILDLIFE OBSERVED:

POPULAR ATTRACTIONS I VISITED/EXPERIENCED:

- [ ] RIM DRIVE
- [ ] WIZARD ISLAND
- [ ] SUN NOTCH TRAIL
- [ ] CLEETWOOD COVE TRAIL
- [ ] PLAIKNI FALLS
- [ ] CRATER LAKE LODGE
- [ ] GARFIELD PEAK
- [ ] SINNOTT MEMORIAL OVERLOOK & RIM WALK
- [ ] PINNACLES OVERLOOK
- [ ] CASTLE CREST WILDFLOWER GARDEN

OVERALL EXPERIENCE

☆

10

CUYAHOGA VALLEY
NATIONAL PARK

◉ CITY/STATE ENTERED:

DATE(S) VISITED:

WEATHER:
_____ °F

COMPANIONS:

LODGING:

FEE(S):

FAVORITE MOMENT:

SIGHTS:

WILDLIFE OBSERVED:

POPULAR ATTRACTIONS I VISITED/EXPERIENCED:

- [ ] BRANDYWINE FALLS
- [ ] BEAVER MARSH
- [ ] PLATEAU TRAIL
- [ ] VALLEY BRIDLE TRAIL
- [ ] KENDALL LAKE LOOP TRAIL
- [ ] BLUE HEN FALLS
- [ ] LEDGES TRAIL
- [ ] THE OHIO & ERIE CANAL TOWPATH TRAIL
- [ ] CANAL EXPLORATION CENTER
- [ ] CUYAHOGA VALLEY SCENIC RAILROAD

OVERALL EXPERIENCE

☆

10

DEATH VALLEY
NATIONAL PARK

⚬ CITY/STATE ENTERED:

📅 DATE(S) VISITED:

WEATHER:
🚩 ☀️ ⛅ 🌧️ ⛈️ ❄️
_____ °F

👥 COMPANIONS:

🏕️ LODGING:

💵 FEE(S):

🥾 FAVORITE MOMENT:

⛰️ SIGHTS:

🐦 WILDLIFE OBSERVED:

POPULAR ATTRACTIONS I VISITED/EXPERIENCED:

- [ ] WILDROSE CHARCOAL KILNS
- [ ] DEVILS GOLF COURSE
- [ ] UBEHEBE CRATER
- [ ] BADWATER BASIN
- [ ] DANTE'S VIEW
- [ ] MESQUITE FLAT SAND DUNES
- [ ] ARTISTS PALETTE
- [ ] RACETRACK PLAYA
- [ ] MOSAIC CANYON TRAIL
- [ ] ZABRISKIE POINT

OVERALL EXPERIENCE

☆

10

DENALI
NATIONAL PARK
◉ CITY/STATE ENTERED:

📅 DATE(S) VISITED:

WEATHER:
°F

👥 COMPANIONS:

🏕 LODGING:

💵 FEE(S):

🥾 FAVORITE MOMENT:

⛰ SIGHTS :

🐦 WILDLIFE OBSERVED:

POPULAR ATTRACTIONS I VISITED/EXPERIENCED:

- ☐ HORSESHOE LAKE TRAIL
- ☐ MT HEALY OVERLOOK TRAIL
- ☐ TRIPLE LAKES TRAIL
- ☐ SAVAGE ALPINE TRAIL
- ☐ SLED DOG KENNELS
- ☐ ROCK CREEK TRAIL
- ☐ MCKINLEY STATION TRAIL
- ☐ WONDER LAKE
- ☐ MT MARGARET SUMMIT
- ☐ SAVAGE RIVER LOOP TRAIL

OVERALL EXPERIENCE
☆

10

DRY TORTUGAS
NATIONAL PARK

📍 CITY/STATE ENTERED:

📅 DATE(S) VISITED:

WEATHER:
_____ °F

👥 COMPANIONS:

🏕 LODGING:

💵 FEE(S):

🥾 FAVORITE MOMENT:

⛰ SIGHTS :

🐦 WILDLIFE OBSERVED:

POPULAR ATTRACTIONS I VISITED/EXPERIENCED:

- [ ] FORT JEFFERSON
- [ ] GARDEN KEY
- [ ] BUSH KEY TRAIL
- [ ] SOUTH SWIM BEACH
- [ ] DRY TORTUGAS LIGHTHOUSE
- [ ] SNORKELING & DIVING
- [ ] LOGGERHEAD KEY
- [ ] TORTUGAS BANKS
- [ ] DINGHY BEACH
- [ ] GREAT FLORIDA BIRDING TRAIL

OVERALL EXPERIENCE
☆

10

EVERGLADES
NATIONAL PARK

◉ CITY/STATE ENTERED:

DATE(S) VISITED:

WEATHER:
°F

COMPANIONS:

LODGING:

FEE(S):

FAVORITE MOMENT:

SIGHTS:

WILDLIFE OBSERVED:

POPULAR ATTRACTIONS I VISITED/EXPERIENCED:

- [ ] TEN THOUSAND ISLANDS
- [ ] SHARK VALLEY
- [ ] NINE MILE POND CANOE TRAIL
- [ ] PA-HAY-OKEE TRAIL
- [ ] MARCO ISLAND
- [ ] ANHINGA TRAIL
- [ ] LOOP ROAD SCENIC DRIVE
- [ ] CHOKOLOSKEE BAY
- [ ] CORKSCREW SWAMP SANCTUARY
- [ ] BIG CYPRESS NATIONAL PRESERVE

OVERALL EXPERIENCE

☆

10

GATES OF THE ARCTIC
NATIONAL PARK

◉ CITY/STATE ENTERED:

DATE(S) VISITED:

WEATHER:
°F

COMPANIONS:

LODGING:

FEE(S):

FAVORITE MOMENT:

SIGHTS :

WILDLIFE OBSERVED:

POPULAR ATTRACTIONS I VISITED/EXPERIENCED:

- [ ] ARRIGETCH PEAKS
- [ ] TAKAHULA LAKE
- [ ] MOUNT IGIKPAK
- [ ] BOREAL MOUNTAIN
- [ ] KOYUKUK RIVER
- [ ] FRIGID CRAGS
- [ ] ALATNA NATIONAL WILD & SCENIC RIVER
- [ ] WALKER LAKE
- [ ] TINAYGUK RIVER
- [ ] KOBUK WILD RIVER

OVERALL EXPERIENCE
☆

10

GATEWAY ARCH
NATIONAL PARK

📍 CITY/STATE ENTERED:

📅 DATE(S) VISITED:

WEATHER:

_____ °F

👥 COMPANIONS:

🏕 LODGING:

💵 FEE(S):

🥾 FAVORITE MOMENT:

⛰ SIGHTS :

🐦 WILDLIFE OBSERVED:

POPULAR ATTRACTIONS I VISITED/EXPERIENCED:

- [ ] GATEWAY ARCH & MUSEUM
- [ ] OLD COURTHOUSE
- [ ] CITY MUSEUM
- [ ] CITY GARDEN
- [ ] PARK BIKING / WALKING PATHS
- [ ] MISSISSIPI CRUISING
- [ ] MUSEUM OF WESTWARD EXPANSION
- [ ] HISTORICAL PANELS
- [ ] DINING WITH A VIEW
- [ ] ....

OVERALL EXPERIENCE

☆

10

GLACIER
NATIONAL PARK

○ CITY/STATE ENTERED:

DATE(S) VISITED:

WEATHER:
_____ °F

COMPANIONS:

LODGING:

FEE(S):

FAVORITE MOMENT:

SIGHTS:

WILDLIFE OBSERVED:

POPULAR ATTRACTIONS I VISITED/EXPERIENCED:

- [ ] LAKE MCDONALD
- [ ] TRAIL OF THE CEDARS
- [ ] ST. MARY FALLS
- [ ] ICEBERG LAKE TRAIL
- [ ] WILD GOOSE ISLAND LOOKOUT
- [ ] HIGHLINE TRAIL
- [ ] GOING-TO-THE-SUN ROAD
- [ ] GRINNELL LAKE & BOAT TOUR
- [ ] AVALANCHE LAKE
- [ ] HIDDEN LAKE OVERLOOK

OVERALL EXPERIENCE

☆

10

GLACIER BAY NATIONAL PARK

○ CITY/STATE ENTERED:

📅 DATE(S) VISITED:

WEATHER:
°F

👥 COMPANIONS:

🏕 LODGING:

💰 FEE(S):

⛰ FAVORITE MOMENT:

🏔 SIGHTS:

🐦 WILDLIFE OBSERVED:

POPULAR ATTRACTIONS I VISITED/EXPERIENCED:

- [ ] BEACH TRAIL
- [ ] BARTLETT LAKE TRAIL
- [ ] BARTLETT RIVER TRAIL
- [ ] SEBREE ISLAND
- [ ] FOREST LOOP TRAIL
- [ ] TLINGIT TRAIL
- [ ] MARGERIE GLACIER
- [ ] HALIBUT POINT WHALE WATCHING
- [ ] BARTLETT COVE KAYAKING
- [ ] JOHNS HOPKINS GLACIER

OVERALL EXPERIENCE

☆

10

GRAND CANYON
NATIONAL PARK

◉ CITY/STATE ENTERED:

📅 DATE(S) VISITED:

WEATHER:
°F

👥 COMPANIONS:

🏕 LODGING:

💵 FEE(S):

🥾 FAVORITE MOMENT:

⛰ SIGHTS :

🦅 WILDLIFE OBSERVED:

POPULAR ATTRACTIONS I VISITED/EXPERIENCED:

- ☐ DESERT VIEW DRIVE
- ☐ BRIGHT ANGEL TRAIL
- ☐ NORTH KAIBAB TRAIL
- ☐ DESERT VIEW WATCHTOWER
- ☐ MATHER POINT OVERLOOK
- ☐ NORTH RIM SCENIC DRIVE
- ☐ RIM TRAIL
- ☐ HAVASU FALLS
- ☐ GRAND CANYON RAILWAY
- ☐ HERMIT ROAD

OVERALL EXPERIENCE
☆

10

GRAND TETON
NATIONAL PARK

○ CITY/STATE ENTERED:

DATE(S) VISITED:

WEATHER:

_____ °F

COMPANIONS:

LODGING:

FEE(S):

FAVORITE MOMENT:

SIGHTS:

WILDLIFE OBSERVED:

POPULAR ATTRACTIONS I VISITED/EXPERIENCED:

- [ ] JENNY LAKE TRAIL
- [ ] SNAKE RIVER OVERLOOK
- [ ] SCHWABACHER'S LANDING
- [ ] STRING LAKE
- [ ] MOOSE WILSON ROAD
- [ ] 42-MILE SCENIC LOOP DRIVE
- [ ] TAGGART LAKE TRAIL
- [ ] OXBOW BEND
- [ ] MORMON ROW HISTORIC DISTRICT
- [ ] INSPIRATION POINT

OVERALL EXPERIENCE

☆

10

GREAT BASIN
NATIONAL PARK

○ CITY/STATE ENTERED:

DATE(S) VISITED:

WEATHER:

_____ °F

COMPANIONS:

LODGING:

FEE(S):

FAVORITE MOMENT:

SIGHTS :

WILDLIFE OBSERVED:

POPULAR ATTRACTIONS I VISITED/EXPERIENCED:

- [ ] LEHMAN CAVES
- [ ] BRISTLECONE TRAILS
- [ ] STELLA LAKE
- [ ] MATHER OVERLOOK
- [ ] LEHMAN CREEK TRAIL
- [ ] WHEELER PEAK
- [ ] ALPINE LAKES LOOP
- [ ] TERESA LAKE
- [ ] BAKER LAKE TRAIL
- [ ] SUMMIT TRAIL

OVERALL EXPERIENCE

☆

10

GREAT SAND DUNES NATIONAL PARK

○ CITY/STATE ENTERED:

DATE(S) VISITED:

WEATHER:
_____ °F

👥 COMPANIONS:

🏕 LODGING:

💰 FEE(S):

🥾 FAVORITE MOMENT:

⛰ SIGHTS :

🦅 WILDLIFE OBSERVED:

POPULAR ATTRACTIONS I VISITED/EXPERIENCED:

- ☐ ZAPATA FALLS
- ☐ MEDANO PASS PRIMITIVE ROAD
- ☐ MOSCA PASS TRAIL
- ☐ MEDANO CREEK
- ☐ SAND SLEDDING
- ☐ HIGH DUNE
- ☐ ZAPATA FALLS
- ☐ MONTVILLE NATURE TRAIL
- ☐ BACA NATIONAL WILDLIFE REFUGE
- ☐ DUNES TRAIL FROM PINYON FLATS

OVERALL EXPERIENCE

☆

10

GREAT SMOKY MOUNTAINS NATIONAL PARK

○ CITY/STATE ENTERED:

DATE(S) VISITED:

WEATHER:
_____ °F

COMPANIONS:

LODGING:

FEE(S):

FAVORITE MOMENT:

SIGHTS :

WILDLIFE OBSERVED:

POPULAR ATTRACTIONS I VISITED/EXPERIENCED:

- [ ] NEWFOUND GAP ROAD
- [ ] MINGUS MILL
- [ ] APPALACHIAN TRAIL
- [ ] GROTTO FALLS TRAIL
- [ ] ALUM CAVE TRAIL
- [ ] CADES COVE
- [ ] ROARING FORK MOTOR NATURE TRAIL
- [ ] CLINGMANS DOME
- [ ] LAUREL FALLS
- [ ] ELKMONT HISTORIC DISTRICT

OVERALL EXPERIENCE

☆

10

GUADALUPE MOUNTAINS
NATIONAL PARK

⊙ CITY/STATE ENTERED:

📅 DATE(S) VISITED:

WEATHER:
°F

👥 COMPANIONS:

🏕 LODGING:

💵 FEE(S):

🥾 FAVORITE MOMENT:

⛰ SIGHTS :

🐦 WILDLIFE OBSERVED:

POPULAR ATTRACTIONS I VISITED/EXPERIENCED:

- [ ] GUADALUPE PEAK
- [ ] DEVIL'S HALL TRAIL
- [ ] SMITH SPRING
- [ ] PERMIAN REEF GEOLOGY TRAIL
- [ ] DOG CANYON
- [ ] MCKITTRICK CANYON
- [ ] EL CAPITAN
- [ ] PINERY NATURE TRAIL
- [ ] SALT BASIN DUNES
- [ ] FRIJOLE RANCH

OVERALL EXPERIENCE
☆

10

HALEAKALĀ
NATIONAL PARK

◉ CITY/STATE ENTERED:

DATE(S) VISITED:

WEATHER:
_____ °F

COMPANIONS:

LODGING:

FEE(S):

FAVORITE MOMENT:

SIGHTS:

WILDLIFE OBSERVED:

POPULAR ATTRACTIONS I VISITED/EXPERIENCED:

- [ ] HĀNA HIGHWAY
- [ ] PIPIWAI TRAIL
- [ ] 'OHEO' GULCH
- [ ] POOLS OF 'OHEO'
- [ ] MAKAHIKU FALLS
- [ ] HALEAKALĀ CRATER
- [ ] SLIDING SANDS TRAIL
- [ ] HALEAKALĀ OBSERVATORIES
- [ ] WAIMOKU FALLS
- [ ] SUPPLY TRAIL

OVERALL EXPERIENCE
☆

10

HAWAI'I VOLCANOES
NATIONAL PARK

📍 CITY/STATE ENTERED:

📅 DATE(S) VISITED:

WEATHER:
_____ °F

👥 COMPANIONS:

🏕 LODGING:

💵 FEE(S):

🥾 FAVORITE MOMENT:

⛰ SIGHTS :

🐦 WILDLIFE OBSERVED:

POPULAR ATTRACTIONS I VISITED/EXPERIENCED:

- [ ] KĪLAUEA IKI TRAIL
- [ ] KALAPANA
- [ ] PU'U LOA PETROGLYPHS
- [ ] DEVASTATION TRAIL
- [ ] JAGGA MUSEUM & OVERLOOK
- [ ] CHAIN OF THE CRATERS ROAD
- [ ] HOLEI SEA ARCH
- [ ] HALEMA'UMA'U CRATER
- [ ] THURSTON LAVA TUBE
- [ ] KIPUKA PUAULA BIRD PARK

OVERALL EXPERIENCE
☆

10

HOT SPRINGS
NATICNAL PARK

◉ CITY/STATE ENTERED:

📅 DATE(S) VISITED:

WEATHER:
🚩 ☀️ ⛅ 🌧️ ⛈️ ❄️
_____ °F

👥 COMPANIONS:

🏕️ LODGING:

💰 FEE(S):

🥾 FAVORITE MOMENT:

⛰️ SIGHTS :

🐦 WILDLIFE OBSERVED:

POPULAR ATTRACTIONS I VISITED/EXPERIENCED:

- ☐ FORDYCE BATTHOUSE
- ☐ BATHHOUSE ROW
- ☐ BUCKSTAFF BATHHOUSE
- ☐ SUNSET TRAIL
- ☐ LAKE OUACHITA
- ☐ GARVAN WOODLANDS GARDENS
- ☐ GRAND PROMENADE
- ☐ SUPERIOR BATHHOUSE BREWERY
- ☐ HOT SPRINGS MOUNTAIN LOOP
- ☐ ANTHONY CHAPEL

OVERALL EXPERIENCE

☆

10

INDIANA DUNES
NATIONAL PARK

📍 CITY/STATE ENTERED:

📅 DATE(S) VISITED:

WEATHER:
_____ °F

👥 COMPANIONS:

⛺ LODGING:

💵 FEE(S):

🥾 FAVORITE MOMENT:

⛰ SIGHTS :

🐦 WILDLIFE OBSERVED:

POPULAR ATTRACTIONS I VISITED/EXPERIENCED:

- [ ] LAKE VIEW BEACH
- [ ] COWLES BOG TRAIL
- [ ] MOUNT BALDY
- [ ] OGDEN DUNES BEACH
- [ ] DEEP RIVER WATERPARK
- [ ] TALTREE ARBORETUM & GARDENS
- [ ] PINE LAKE
- [ ] PORTAGE LAKEFRONT & RIVERWALK TRAIL
- [ ] COFFEE CREEK WATERSHED PRESERVE
- [ ] WEST BEACH 3-LOOP TRAIL

OVERALL EXPERIENCE
☆

10

ISLE ROYALE
NATIONAL PARK

◉ CITY/STATE ENTERED:

DATE(S) VISITED:

WEATHER:
___ °F

👥 COMPANIONS:

🏕 LODGING:

💵 FEE(S):

🥾 FAVORITE MOMENT:

⛰ SIGHTS :

🦅 WILDLIFE OBSERVED:

POPULAR ATTRACTIONS I VISITED/EXPERIENCED:

- [ ] ROCK HARBOR
- [ ] GREENSTONE RIDGE TRAIL
- [ ] ROCK ISLAND LIGHTHOUSE
- [ ] MOUNT OJIBWAY TRAIL
- [ ] WINDIGO
- [ ] SCOVILLE POINT
- [ ] SUZY'S CAVE
- [ ] LOOKOUT LOUISE
- [ ] PASSAGE ISLAND
- [ ] CHICKENBONE LAKE

OVERALL EXPERIENCE
☆

10

JOSHUA TREE
NATIONAL PARK

◦ CITY/STATE ENTERED:

📅 DATE(S) VISITED:

WEATHER:
°F

👥 COMPANIONS:

🏕 LODGING:

💰 FEE(S):

🥾 FAVORITE MOMENT:

⛰ SIGHTS :

🐦 WILDLIFE OBSERVED:

POPULAR ATTRACTIONS I VISITED/EXPERIENCED:

- [ ] BARRAGE BARKER
- [ ] COACHELLA VALLEY PRESERVE
- [ ] KEYS VIEW
- [ ] BARKER DAM TRAIL
- [ ] 49 PALMS CANYON TRAIL
- [ ] SKULL ROCK
- [ ] CHOLLA CACTUS GARDEN
- [ ] HIDDEN VALLEY NATURE TRAIL
- [ ] RYAN MOUNTAIN
- [ ] CAP ROCK

OVERALL EXPERIENCE

☆

10

KATMAI NATIONAL PARK

○ CITY/STATE ENTERED:

DATE(S) VISITED:

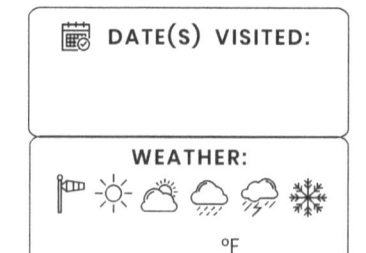

WEATHER:
____ °F

COMPANIONS:

LODGING:

FEE(S):

FAVORITE MOMENT:

SIGHTS:

WILDLIFE OBSERVED:

POPULAR ATTRACTIONS I VISITED/EXPERIENCED:

- ☐ BROOKS FALLS
- ☐ BROOKS RIVER
- ☐ NAKNEK LAKE
- ☐ NOVARUPTA
- ☐ FALLING MOUNTAIN
- ☐ VALLEY OF TEN THOUSAND SMOKES
- ☐ MOUNT KATMAI
- ☐ HALLO BAY
- ☐ SAVONOSKI LOOP
- ☐ MCNEIL RIVER STATE GAME SANCTUARY

OVERALL EXPERIENCE

☆

10

KENAI FJORDS NATIONAL PARK

○ CITY/STATE ENTERED:

DATE(S) VISITED:

WEATHER:
_____ °F

COMPANIONS:

LODGING:

FEE(S):

FAVORITE MOMENT:

SIGHTS:

WILDLIFE OBSERVED:

POPULAR ATTRACTIONS I VISITED/EXPERIENCED:

- [ ] EXIT GLACIER
- [ ] FOX ISLAND
- [ ] PEDERSON GLACIER
- [ ] TONSINA POINT
- [ ] KACHEMAK BAY STATE PARK
- [ ] HARDING ICE FIELD TRAIL
- [ ] SIX MILE CREEK
- [ ] AIALIK GLACIER
- [ ] BOAT TOURS
- [ ] GREWINGK GLACIER LAKE TRAIL

OVERALL EXPERIENCE

☆

10

KINGS CANYON
NATIONAL PARK

⚬ CITY/STATE ENTERED:

📅 DATE(S) VISITED:

WEATHER:

___°F

👥 COMPANIONS:

🏕 LODGING:

💰 FEE(S):

🥾 FAVORITE MOMENT:

⛰ SIGHTS :

🐦 WILDLIFE OBSERVED:

POPULAR ATTRACTIONS I VISITED/EXPERIENCED:

- [ ] GENERAL GRANT GROVE
- [ ] GRIZZLY FALLS
- [ ] MIST FALLS TRAIL
- [ ] RAE LAKES TRAIL
- [ ] HUME LAKE
- [ ] ROARING RIVER FALLS
- [ ] KINGS CANYON SCENIC BYWAY
- [ ] BUENA VISTA PEAK
- [ ] BIG STUMP TRAIL
- [ ] ZUMWALT MEADOW

OVERALL EXPERIENCE

☆

10

KOBUK VALLEY
NATIONAL PARK

◉ CITY/STATE ENTERED:

📅 DATE(S) VISITED:

WEATHER:
_____ °F

COMPANIONS:

LODGING:

FEE(S):

FAVORITE MOMENT:

SIGHTS:

WILDLIFE OBSERVED:

POPULAR ATTRACTIONS I VISITED/EXPERIENCED:

- ☐ GREAT KOBUK SAND DUNES
- ☐ ONION PORTAGE
- ☐ LITTLE KOBUK SAND DUNES
- ☐ BAIRD MOUNTAINS
- ☐ ANGAYUKAQSRAQ PEAK
- ☐ AHNEWETUT CREEK
- ☐ RAFTING
- ☐ HUNT RIVER DUNES
- ☐ KOTZEBUE
- ☐ SALMON RIVER

OVERALL EXPERIENCE

☆

10

LAKE CLARK
NATICIONAL PARK

○ CITY/STATE ENTERED:

DATE(S) VISITED:

WEATHER:
___ °F

COMPANIONS:

LODGING:

FEE(S):

FAVORITE MOMENT:

SIGHTS:

WILDLIFE OBSERVED:

POPULAR ATTRACTIONS I VISITED/EXPERIENCED:

- ☐ TURQUOISE LAKE
- ☐ MULCHATNA RIVER
- ☐ TLIKAKILA RIVER
- ☐ CHIGMIT MOUNTAINS
- ☐ KONTRASHIBUNA LAKE
- ☐ CHILIKADROTNA RIVER
- ☐ TURQUOISE VALLEY
- ☐ LAKE CLARK
- ☐ TANALIAN FALLS
- ☐ TANALIAN MOUNTAIN

OVERALL EXPERIENCE
☆

10

LASSEN VOLCANIC NATIONAL PARK

○ CITY/STATE ENTERED:

DATE(S) VISITED:

WEATHER:
____ °F

COMPANIONS:

LODGING:

FEE(S):

FAVORITE MOMENT:

SIGHTS :

WILDLIFE OBSERVED:

POPULAR ATTRACTIONS I VISITED/EXPERIENCED:

- ☐ MANZANITA LAKE
- ☐ LAKE HELEN
- ☐ BUMPASS HELL
- ☐ KINGS CREEK FALLS
- ☐ MOUNT LASSEN
- ☐ SULPHUR WORKS
- ☐ DEVASTATED AREA
- ☐ SUMMIT LAKE
- ☐ HAT CREEK
- ☐ CINDER CONE

OVERALL EXPERIENCE
☆

10

MAMMOTH CAVE
NATIONAL PARK

○ CITY/STATE ENTERED:

DATE(S) VISITED:

WEATHER:
°F

COMPANIONS:

LODGING:

FEE(S):

FAVORITE MOMENT:

SIGHTS:

WILDLIFE OBSERVED:

POPULAR ATTRACTIONS I VISITED/EXPERIENCED:

- ☐ DIAMOND CAVERNS
- ☐ SLOAN'S CROSSING POND
- ☐ RIVER STYX SPRING
- ☐ CEDAR SINK TRAIL
- ☐ TURNHOLE BEND NATURE TRAILHEAD
- ☐ MAMMOTH CAVE
- ☐ GREEN RIVER BLUFFS TRAIL
- ☐ HERITAGE TRAIL
- ☐ RAILROAD HIKE & BIKE TRAIL
- ☐ NOLIN LAKE

OVERALL EXPERIENCE

☆

10

MESA VERDE
NATIONAL PARK

◉ CITY/STATE ENTERED:

📅 DATE(S) VISITED:

WEATHER:
🚩 ☀️ ☁️ 🌧️ ⛈️ ❄️
_____ °F

👥 COMPANIONS:

⛺ LODGING:

💵 FEE(S):

🥾 FAVORITE MOMENT:

⛰️ SIGHTS:

🐦 WILDLIFE OBSERVED:

POPULAR ATTRACTIONS I VISITED/EXPERIENCED:

- ☐ CLIFF PALACE
- ☐ SPRUCE TREE HOUSE
- ☐ SQUARE TOWER HOUSE
- ☐ CHAPIN MESA MUSEUM
- ☐ PRATER EDGE TRAIL
- ☐ BALCONY HOUSE
- ☐ MESA TOP LOOP
- ☐ LONG HOUSE
- ☐ PETROGLYPH POINT TRAIL
- ☐ FAR VIEW RUINS

OVERALL EXPERIENCE
☆

10

MOUNT RAINIER
NATIONAL PARK

⊙ CITY/STATE ENTERED:

📅 DATE(S) VISITED:

WEATHER: 🚩 ☀️ ⛅ 🌧️ ⛈️ ❄️
_____ °F

👥 **COMPANIONS:**

🏕️ **LODGING:**

💲 **FEE(S):**

🥾 **FAVORITE MOMENT:**

⛰️ **SIGHTS :**

🐦 **WILDLIFE OBSERVED:**

POPULAR ATTRACTIONS I VISITED/EXPERIENCED:

- ☐ SKYLINE TRAIL
- ☐ NARADA FALLS
- ☐ REFLECTION LAKES
- ☐ COMET FALLS
- ☐ TIPSOO LAKE
- ☐ SNOW LAKE
- ☐ LONGMIRE
- ☐ MYRTLE FALLS
- ☐ GROVE OF THE PATRIARCHS
- ☐ SOURDOUGH RIDGE NATURE TRAIL

OVERALL EXPERIENCE
☆

10

NORTH CASCADES
NATIONAL PARK

📍 CITY/STATE ENTERED:

📅 DATE(S) VISITED:

WEATHER:
_____ °F

👥 COMPANIONS:

🏕 LODGING:

💰 FEE(S):

🥾 FAVORITE MOMENT:

⛰ SIGHTS:

🐦 WILDLIFE OBSERVED:

POPULAR ATTRACTIONS I VISITED/EXPERIENCED:

- [ ] DIABLO LAKE OVERLOOK
- [ ] RAINY LAKE
- [ ] THUNDER KNOB
- [ ] STEHEKIN
- [ ] MOUNT SHUKSAN
- [ ] LADDER CREEK FALLS
- [ ] STERLING MUNRO TRAIL
- [ ] CASCADE PASS TRAILHEAD
- [ ] WASHINGTON PASS OVERLOOK
- [ ] ROSS DAM TRAIL

OVERALL EXPERIENCE
☆

10

OLYMPIC
NATIONAL PARK

⦿ CITY/STATE ENTERED:

📅 DATE(S) VISITED:

WEATHER:
🚩 ☀️ ⛅ 🌧️ ⛈️ ❄️
_____ °F

👥 COMPANIONS:

⛺ LODGING:

💵 FEE(S):

🥾 FAVORITE MOMENT:

⛰️ SIGHTS :

🦅 WILDLIFE OBSERVED:

🌲 POPULAR ATTRACTIONS I VISITED/EXPERIENCED:

- [ ] RIALTO BEACH
- [ ] LAKE CRESCENT
- [ ] RUBY BEACH
- [ ] HIGH RIDGE TRAIL
- [ ] KALALOCH BEACH 4
- [ ] HURRICANE HILL TRAIL
- [ ] MADISON FALLS
- [ ] HALL OF MOSSES
- [ ] SOL DUC FALLS
- [ ] MARYMERE FALLS

OVERALL EXPERIENCE
☆

10

PETRIFIED FOREST
NATICCITY/STATE ENTERED:

DATE(S) VISITED:

WEATHER:
°F

COMPANIONS:

LODGING:

FEE(S):

FAVORITE MOMENT:

SIGHTS:

WILDLIFE OBSERVED:

POPULAR ATTRACTIONS I VISITED/EXPERIENCED:

- [ ] CRYSTAL FOREST TRAIL
- [ ] BLUE MESA TRAIL
- [ ] ROUTE 66
- [ ] JASPER FOREST
- [ ] RAINBOW FOREST
- [ ] PAINTED DESERT RIM TRAIL
- [ ] GIANT LOGS TRAIL
- [ ] PUERCO PUEBLO & NEWSPAPER ROCK
- [ ] LONG LOGS & AGATE HOUSE LOOP
- [ ] OFF-THE-BEATEN-PATH HIKE

OVERALL EXPERIENCE

☆

10

PINNACLES
NATIONAL PARK

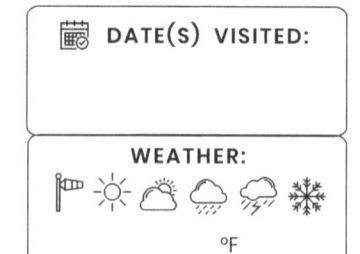

○ CITY/STATE ENTERED:

DATE(S) VISITED:

WEATHER:
___ °F

COMPANIONS:

LODGING:

FEE(S):

FAVORITE MOMENT:

SIGHTS:

WILDLIFE OBSERVED:

POPULAR ATTRACTIONS I VISITED/EXPERIENCED:

- [ ] BEAR GULCH CAVE TRAIL
- [ ] BALCONIES CAVE TRAIL
- [ ] JUNIPER CANYON LOOP
- [ ] BEAR GULCH RESERVOIR
- [ ] ROCK CLIMBING
- [ ] HIGH PEAKS TRAIL
- [ ] CONDOR GULCH TRAIL
- [ ] MOSES SPRING TRAIL
- [ ] CHALONE PEAK TRAIL
- [ ] BIRD WATCHING

OVERALL EXPERIENCE
☆

10

REDWOOD
NATIONAL PARK

◎ CITY/STATE ENTERED:

DATE(S) VISITED:

WEATHER:
_____ °F

COMPANIONS:

LODGING:

FEE(S):

FAVORITE MOMENT:

SIGHTS :

WILDLIFE OBSERVED:

POPULAR ATTRACTIONS I VISITED/EXPERIENCED:

- [ ] LADY BIRD JOHNSON GROVE
- [ ] BIG TREE
- [ ] TRILLIUM FALLS
- [ ] TALL TREES GROVE
- [ ] GOLD BLUFFS
- [ ] KLAMATH RIVER OVERLOOK
- [ ] COASTAL DRIVE
- [ ] FERN CANYON
- [ ] HOWLAND HILL ROAD
- [ ] STOUT GROVE

OVERALL EXPERIENCE

☆

10

ROCKY MOUNTAIN
NATIONAL PARK
○ CITY/STATE ENTERED:

📅 DATE(S) VISITED:

WEATHER:
____ °F

👥 COMPANIONS:

🏕 LODGING:

💰 FEE(S):

🥾 FAVORITE MOMENT:

⛰ SIGHTS :

🐦 WILDLIFE OBSERVED:

POPULAR ATTRACTIONS I VISITED/EXPERIENCED:

- [ ] TRAIL RIDGE ROAD
- [ ] ALBERTA FALLS
- [ ] OLD FALL RIVER ROAD
- [ ] BIERSTADT LAKE
- [ ] BEAR LAKE
- [ ] EMERALD LAKE
- [ ] TUNDRA COMMUNITIES TRAIL
- [ ] FOREST CANYON OVERLOOK
- [ ] HOLZWARTH HISTORIC SITE
- [ ] COYOTE VALLEY NATURE TRAIL

OVERALL EXPERIENCE
☆

10

SAGUARO NATIONAL PARK

· · · · ·

◎ CITY/STATE ENTERED:

📅 DATE(S) VISITED:

WEATHER:
🚩 ☀️ ⛅ 🌧️ ⛈️ ❄️
_____ °F

👥 COMPANIONS:

🏕️ LODGING:

💵 FEE(S):

🥾 FAVORITE MOMENT:

⛰️ SIGHTS :

🐦 WILDLIFE OBSERVED:

🌵 POPULAR ATTRACTIONS I VISITED/EXPERIENCED:

- [ ] VALLEY VIEW OVERLOOK
- [ ] MICA VIEW LOOP
- [ ] LOMA VERDE TRAIL
- [ ] BAJADA LOOP DRIVE
- [ ] WASSON PEAK
- [ ] SIGNAL HILLS PETROGLYPHS
- [ ] DESERT DISCOVERY NATURE TRAIL
- [ ] CACTUS FOREST LOOP DRIVE
- [ ] ARIZONA-SONORA DESERT MUSEUM
- [ ] GATES PASS

OVERALL EXPERIENCE

☆

10

SEQUOIA
NATIONAL PARK

⌖ CITY/STATE ENTERED:

📅 DATE(S) VISITED:

WEATHER:
°F

👥 COMPANIONS:

⛺ LODGING:

💵 FEE(S):

🥾 FAVORITE MOMENT:

⛰ SIGHTS :

🦅 WILDLIFE OBSERVED:

POPULAR ATTRACTIONS I VISITED/EXPERIENCED:

- [ ] GIANT FOREST
- [ ] CONGRESS TRAIL
- [ ] CRYSTAL CAVE
- [ ] BIG TREES TRAIL
- [ ] HIGH SIERRA TRAIL
- [ ] GENERAL SHERMAN TREE
- [ ] MORO ROCK
- [ ] TUNNEL LOG
- [ ] CRESCENT MEADOW/THARP'S LOG
- [ ] TOKOPAH FALLS

OVERALL EXPERIENCE
☆

10

SHENANDOAH
NATIONAL PARK

◉ CITY/STATE ENTERED:

📅 DATE(S) VISITED:

WEATHER:
°F

👥 COMPANIONS:

🏕 LODGING:

💵 FEE(S):

🥾 FAVORITE MOMENT:

⛰ SIGHTS:

🐦 WILDLIFE OBSERVED:

POPULAR ATTRACTIONS I VISITED/EXPERIENCED:

- [ ] HAWKSBILL SUMMIT
- [ ] BYRD VISITOR CENTER
- [ ] DARK HOLLOW FALLS
- [ ] MARY'S ROCK
- [ ] BLACKROCK SUMMIT
- [ ] RANGE VIEW OVERLOOK
- [ ] STONY MAN MOUNTAIN
- [ ] BEARFENCE MOUNTAIN LOOP
- [ ] SAWMILL RUN OVERLOOK
- [ ] WHITEOAK CANYON TRAIL

OVERALL EXPERIENCE

☆

10

THEODORE ROOSEVELT
NATIONAL PARK

○ CITY/STATE ENTERED:

DATE(S) VISITED:

WEATHER:
_____ °F

COMPANIONS:

LODGING:

FEE(S):

FAVORITE MOMENT:

SIGHTS:

WILDLIFE OBSERVED:

POPULAR ATTRACTIONS I VISITED/EXPERIENCED:

- [ ] SPERATI POINT
- [ ] BUCK HILL
- [ ] PETRIFIED FOREST TRAIL
- [ ] OXBOW OVERLOOK
- [ ] CAPROCK-COULEE TRAIL
- [ ] RIVER BEND OVERLOOK
- [ ] LITTLE MO NATURE TRAIL
- [ ] WIND CANYON TRAIL
- [ ] PAINTED CANYON OVERLOOK
- [ ] MALTESE CROSS CABIN

OVERALL EXPERIENCE

☆

10

US VIRGIN ISLANDS
NATIONAL PARK

📍 CITY/STATE ENTERED:

📅 DATE(S) VISITED:

WEATHER:
_____ °F

👥 COMPANIES:

⛺ LODGING:

💰 FEE(S):

🥾 FAVORITE MOMENT:

⛰ SIGHTS:

🦅 WILDLIFE OBSERVED:

POPULAR ATTRACTIONS I VISITED/EXPERIENCED:

- [ ] TRUNK BAY BEACH
- [ ] WATERLEMON CAY
- [ ] REEF BAY TRAIL
- [ ] JUMBIE BEACH
- [ ] HONEYMOON BEACH
- [ ] CINNAMON BAY
- [ ] HAWKSNEST BEACH
- [ ] SALT POND BAY
- [ ] ANNABERG SUGAR PLANTATION
- [ ] NATIONAL PARK UNDERWATER TRAIL

OVERALL EXPERIENCE

☆

10

VOYAGEURS
NATICNAL PARK
◉ CITY/STATE ENTERED:

DATE(S) VISITED:

WEATHER:
____ °F

COMPANIONS:

LODGING:

FEE(S):

FAVORITE MOMENT:

SIGHTS :

WILDLIFE OBSERVED:

POPULAR ATTRACTIONS I VISITED/EXPERIENCED:

- [ ] RAINY LAKE
- [ ] ELLSWORTH ROCK GARDENS
- [ ] CRANE LAKE
- [ ] VERMILION GORGE
- [ ] SAND POINT LAKE
- [ ] KABETOGAMA PENINSULA
- [ ] NAMAKAN ISLAND
- [ ] LOCATOR LAKE TRAIL
- [ ] ECHO BAY TAIL
- [ ] KETTLE FALLS

OVERALL EXPERIENCE
☆

10

WHITE SANDS
NATIONAL PARK

◉ CITY/STATE ENTERED:

DATE(S) VISITED:

WEATHER:
_____ °F

COMPANIONS:

LODGING:

FEE(S):

FAVORITE MOMENT:

SIGHTS:

WILDLIFE OBSERVED:

POPULAR ATTRACTIONS I VISITED/EXPERIENCED:

- [ ] WHITE SANDS VISITOR CENTER
- [ ] PLAYA TRAIL
- [ ] ALKALI FLAT TRAILHEAD
- [ ] LAKE HOLLOMAN
- [ ] INTERDUNE BOARDWALK
- [ ] DUNE LIFE NATURE TRAIL
- [ ] SAND SLEDDING
- [ ] LAKE LUCERO
- [ ] SUNSET STROLL
- [ ] DUNE DRIVE

OVERALL EXPERIENCE

☆

10

WINDCAVE
NATIONAL PARK

○ CITY/STATE ENTERED:

DATE(S) VISITED:

WEATHER:
_____ °F

COMPANIONS:

LODGING:

FEE(S):

FAVORITE MOMENT:

SIGHTS :

WILDLIFE OBSERVED:

POPULAR ATTRACTIONS I VISITED/EXPERIENCED:

- [ ] RANKIN RIDGE TRAIL
- [ ] PRAIRIE VISTA TRAIL
- [ ] WIND CAVE CANYON
- [ ] LOOKOUT POINT TRAIL
- [ ] ELK MOUNTAIN NATURE TRAIL
- [ ] BISON FLATS
- [ ] NPS5 & NP6 BACKROADS
- [ ] COLD BROOK CANYON TRAIL
- [ ] CENTENNIAL TRAIL #89
- [ ] CAVE TOURS

OVERALL EXPERIENCE
☆

10

WRANGELL - ST. ELIAS
NATIONAL PARK

📍 CITY/STATE ENTERED:

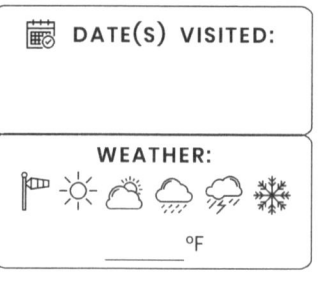

📅 DATE(S) VISITED:

WEATHER:
____ °F

👥 COMPANIONS:

🏕 LODGING:

💰 FEE(S):

🥾 FAVORITE MOMENT:

⛰ SIGHTS:

🐦 WILDLIFE OBSERVED:

POPULAR ATTRACTIONS I VISITED/EXPERIENCED:

- ☐ MOUNT WRANGELL VOLCANO
- ☐ COPPER RIVER TRAIL
- ☐ CHRISTINA RIVER OVERLOOK
- ☐ CHITISTONE CANYON
- ☐ HUBBARD GLACIER
- ☐ NIZINA RIVER BRIDGE
- ☐ JUMBO MINE TRAIL
- ☐ KENNECOTT COPPER MINE
- ☐ ROOT GLACIER TRAIL
- ☐ SKOOKUM VOLCANO TRAIL

OVERALL EXPERIENCE
☆

10

YELLOWSTONE
NATIONAL PARK

◉ CITY/STATE ENTERED:

📅 DATE(S) VISITED:

WEATHER:
_____ °F

👥 COMPANIONS:

🏕 LODGING:

💵 FEE(S):

🥾 FAVORITE MOMENT:

⛰ SIGHTS :

🐦 WILDLIFE OBSERVED:

POPULAR ATTRACTIONS I VISITED/EXPERIENCED:

- ☐ HAYDEN VALLEY
- ☐ MAMMOTH HOT SPRINGS
- ☐ YELLOWSTONE LAKE
- ☐ LAMAR VALLEY
- ☐ TOWER FALL
- ☐ OLD FAITHFUL GEYSER/ UPPER BASIN
- ☐ GRAND CANYON OF THE YELLOWSTONE
- ☐ NORRIS GEYSER BASIN
- ☐ LOWER GEYSER BASIN
- ☐ WEST THUMB GEYSER BASIN

OVERALL EXPERIENCE
☆

10

YOSEMITE
NATIONAL PARK

📍 CITY/STATE ENTERED:

📅 DATE(S) VISITED:

WEATHER:
_____ °F

👥 COMPANIONS:

🏕️ LODGING:

💵 FEE(S):

🥾 FAVORITE MOMENT:

⛰️ SIGHTS:

🐦 WILDLIFE OBSERVED:

POPULAR ATTRACTIONS I VISITED/EXPERIENCED:

- [ ] TUOLUMNE MEADOWS
- [ ] SENTINEL DOME
- [ ] MARIPOSA GROVE
- [ ] VERNAL FALLS
- [ ] TUNNEL VIEW
- [ ] BRIDALVEIL FALLS
- [ ] EL CAPITAN
- [ ] HALF DOME
- [ ] YOSEMITE FALLS
- [ ] GLACIER POINT

OVERALL EXPERIENCE ☆

10

ZION
NATIONAL PARK

⊙ CITY/STATE ENTERED:

📅 DATE(S) VISITED:

WEATHER:

_____ °F

👥 COMPANIONS:

🏕 LODGING:

💰 FEE(S):

🥾 FAVORITE MOMENT:

⛰ SIGHTS :

🐦 WILDLIFE OBSERVED:

POPULAR ATTRACTIONS I VISITED/EXPERIENCED:

- ☐ CANYON OVERLOOK TRAIL
- ☐ CHECKERBOARD MESA
- ☐ THE NARROWS
- ☐ RIVERSIDE WALK
- ☐ OBSERVATION POINT
- ☐ ZION-MOUNT CARMEL HIGHWAY
- ☐ ANGELS LANDING
- ☐ WEEPING ROCK
- ☐ EMERALD POOLS
- ☐ PA'RUS TRAIL

OVERALL EXPERIENCE

☆

10

○○○○○
◎ CITY/STATE ENTERED:

📅 DATE(S) VISITED:

WEATHER:
°F

👥 COMPANIONS:

🏕 LODGING:

💰 FEE(S):

🥾 FAVORITE MOMENT:

⛰ SIGHTS :

🐦 WILDLIFE OBSERVED:

🌲 POPULAR ATTRACTIONS I VISITED/EXPERIENCED:
- [ ]
- [ ]
- [ ]
- [ ]
- [ ]
- [ ]
- [ ]
- [ ]
- [ ]
- [ ]

OVERALL EXPERIENCE
☆

10

CITY/STATE ENTERED:

DATE(S) VISITED:

WEATHER:
°F

COMPANIONS:

LODGING:

FEE(S):

FAVORITE MOMENT:

SIGHTS:

WILDLIFE OBSERVED:

POPULAR ATTRACTIONS I VISITED/EXPERIENCED:
- ☐
- ☐
- ☐
- ☐
- ☐
- ☐
- ☐
- ☐
- ☐
- ☐

OVERALL EXPERIENCE
☆

10

⌖ DATE(S) VISITED:

◉ CITY/STATE ENTERED:

WEATHER:
_____ °F

👥 COMPANIONS:

🏕 LODGING:

💵 FEE(S):

🥾 FAVORITE MOMENT:

⛰ SIGHTS :

🐦 WILDLIFE OBSERVED:

🏞 POPULAR ATTRACTIONS I VISITED/EXPERIENCED:
- [ ]
- [ ]
- [ ]
- [ ]
- [ ]
- [ ]
- [ ]
- [ ]
- [ ]
- [ ]

OVERALL EXPERIENCE
☆

10

CITY/STATE ENTERED:

DATE(S) VISITED:

WEATHER:
_____ °F

COMPANIONS:

LODGING:

FEE(S):

FAVORITE MOMENT:

SIGHTS:

WILDLIFE OBSERVED:

POPULAR ATTRACTIONS I VISITED/EXPERIENCED:
- ☐
- ☐
- ☐
- ☐
- ☐
- ☐
- ☐
- ☐
- ☐
- ☐

OVERALL EXPERIENCE
☆

10

○ CITY/STATE ENTERED:

📅 DATE(S) VISITED:

WEATHER:
🚩 ☀️ ⛅ 🌧️ ⛈️ ❄️
_____ °F

👥 COMPANIONS:

⛺ LODGING:

💰 FEE(S):

🥾 FAVORITE MOMENT:

🏔️ SIGHTS :

🦅 WILDLIFE OBSERVED:

🏞️ POPULAR ATTRACTIONS I VISITED/EXPERIENCED:
☐   ☐
☐   ☐
☐   ☐
☐   ☐
☐   ☐

OVERALL EXPERIENCE
☆

10

WILDLIFE SIGHTINGS

Alaskan Salmon :   Date :
Park :

Alligator :   Date :
Park :

American Bison :   Date :
Park :

American Darter :   Date :
Park :

American Pika :   Date :
Park :

Bald Eagle :   Date :
Park :

Beaver :   Date :
Park :

Bighorn Sheep :   Date :
Park :

Black Bear :   Date :
Park :

Black-Necked Stilt :   Date :
Park :

Black-Tailed Buck :   Date :
Park :

Bobcat :   Date :
Park :

California Condor :   Date :
Park :

California Newt :   Date :
Park :

Caribou :   Date :
Park :

Cedar Waxwing :   Date :
Park :

Chipmunk :   Date :
Park :

Cougar :   Date :
Park :

WILDLIFE SIGHTINGS

Coyote :   Date :
Park :

Dall Sheep :   Date :
Park :

Elephant Seal :   Date :
Park :

Flamingo :   Date :
Park :

Garibaldi Damselfish :   Date :
Park :

Gila Woodpecker :   Date :
Park :

Green Sea Turtle :   Date :
Park :

Grizzly Bear :   Date :
Park :

Hoary Marmot :   Date :
Park :

Horned Toad :   Date :
Park :

Humpback Whale :   Date :
Park :

Moose :   Date :
Park :

Orca :   Date :
Park :

Osprey :   Date :
Park :

Porcupine :   Date :
Park :

Prairie Dog :   Date :
Park :

Pronghorn Antelope :   Date :
Park :

Purple Gallinule :   Date :
Park :

WILDLIFE SIGHTINGS

Purple Swamphen : Date :
Park :

Red-Eared Slider Turtle : Date :
Park :

Red Fox : Date :
Park :

Reddish Egret : Date :
Park :

Rocky Mountain Elk : Date :
Park :

Roosevelt Elk : Date :
Park :

Sandhill Crane : Date :
Park :

Sea Otter : Date :
Park :

Steller Sea Lion : Date :
Park :

Steller's Jay : Date :
Park :

Swift Fox : Date :
Park :

Trumpeter Swan : Date :
Park :

Tufted Puffin : Date :
Park :

Tule Elk : Date :
Park :

Western Scrub-Jays : Date :
Park :

Wild Horse : Date :
Park :

Wild Wolf : Date :
Park :

_____ : Date :
Park :

Made in United States
Troutdale, OR
07/27/2024